Balloon
Trees

by Danna Smith

illustrated by Laurie Allen Klein

This balloon was made from trees—
made from rubber trees like these . . .

The tappers start their work at dawn.
They pull their hats and work gloves on.

They slice the bark then add a spout—
white milky latex drip-drops out.

The simple cup the tappers use collects the natural, sappy ooze.

**From cup to pail to big machine,
this process keeps it soft and clean.**

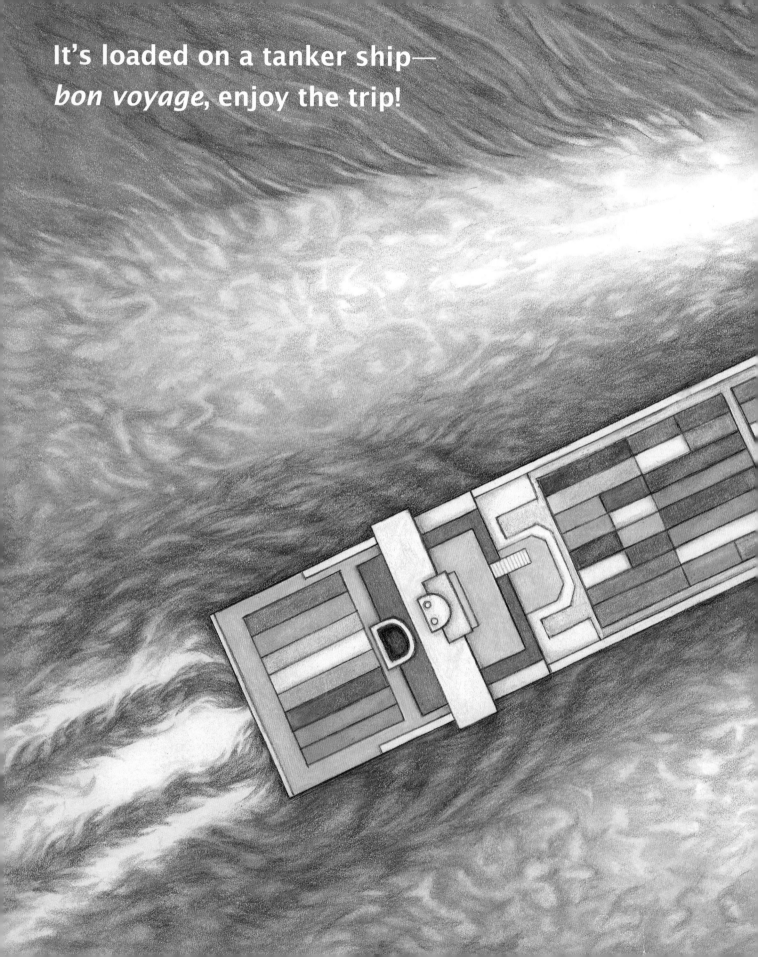

It's loaded on a tanker ship—
bon voyage, enjoy the trip!

A factory waits, with crews and clerks, where loud machines will get to work.

Shipping Invoice

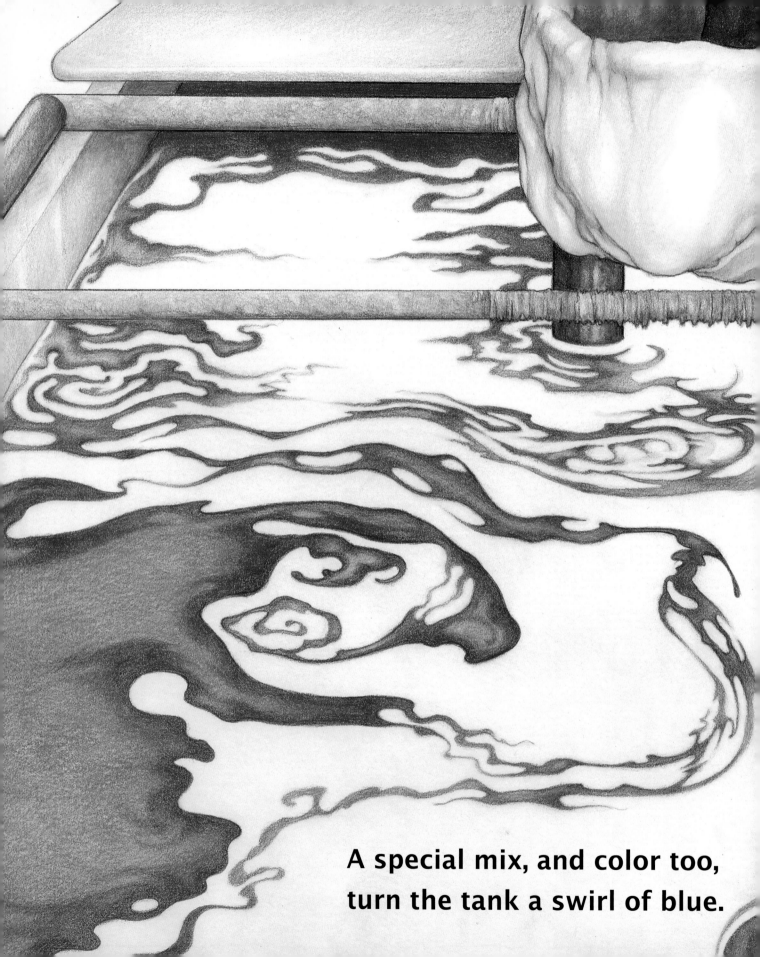

A special mix, and color too,
turn the tank a swirl of blue.

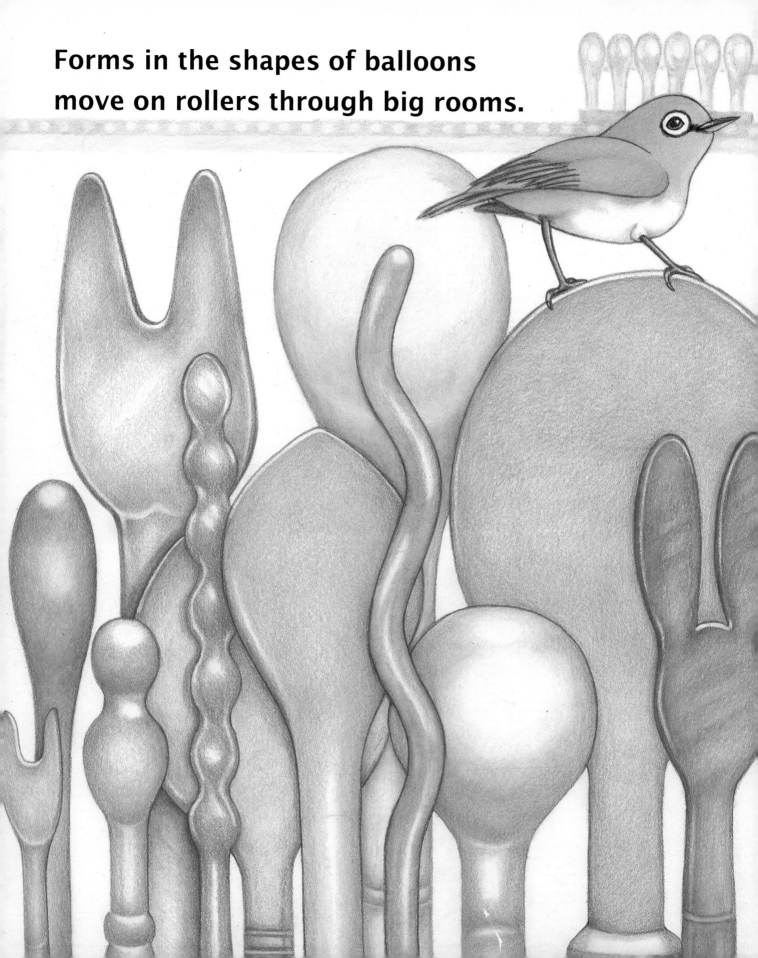

**Forms in the shapes of balloons
move on rollers through big rooms.**

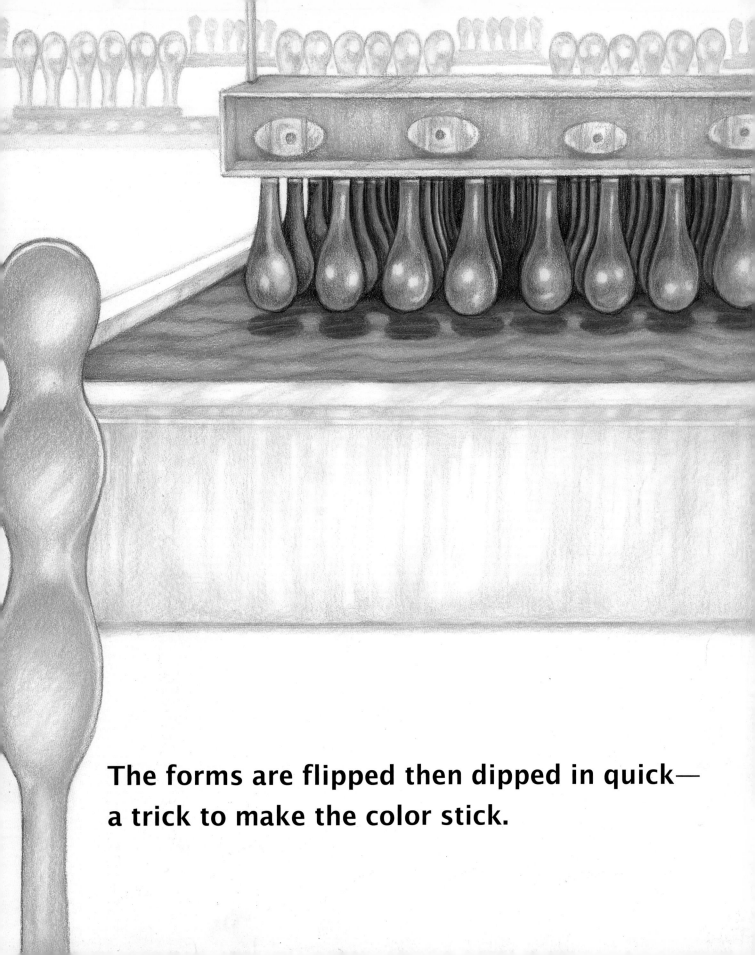

**The forms are flipped then dipped in quick—
a trick to make the color stick.**

The new balloons then make some stops
where spinning brushes roll the tops.

Toward the tub they take a ride.
They soak in water side by side.

Into the oven, they move along—
cooking latex makes it strong.

A dunk in powder . . . in they go—
form by form, row by row.

They're filled with air until they're fat,
then plucked from forms—just like that!

Conveyor belts stay on all day.
They carry bright balloons away.

They travel to a washing machine.
Inside they tumble, squeaky clean.

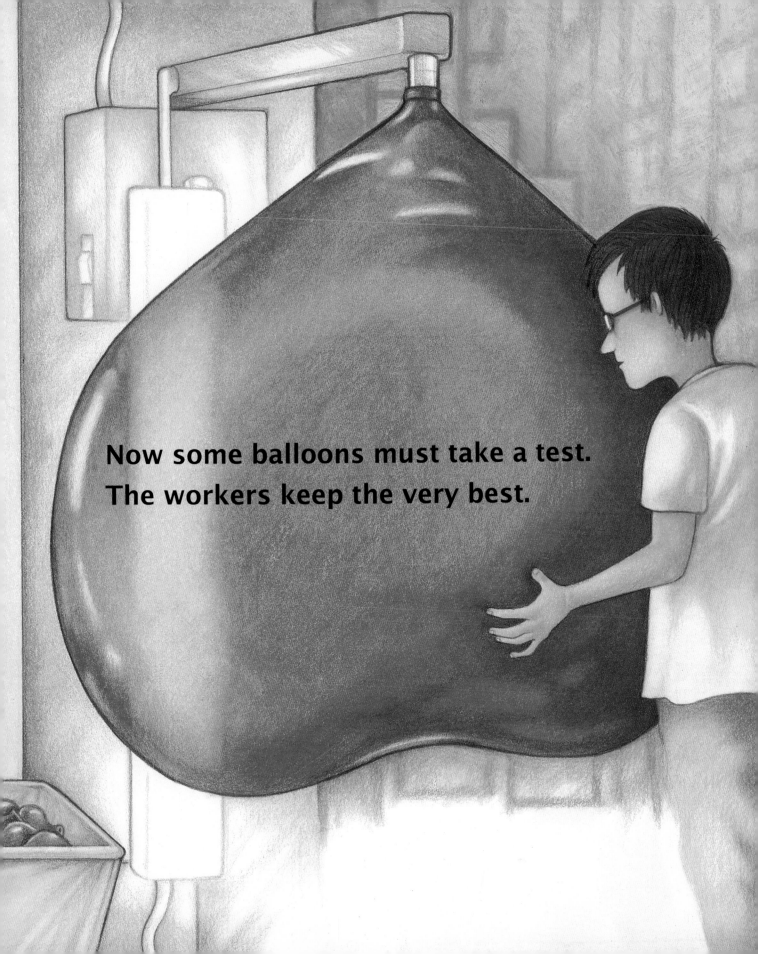

Now some balloons must take a test.
The workers keep the very best.

Bagged and boxed and out the door,
they're taken to your favorite store.

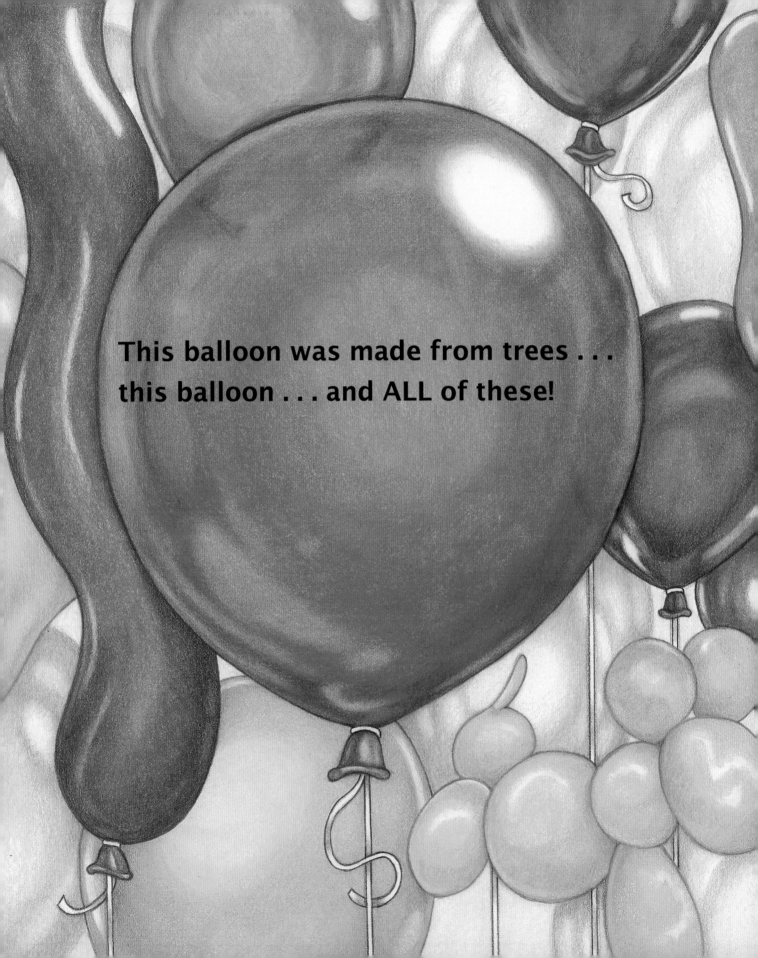

This balloon was made from trees . . .
this balloon . . . and ALL of these!

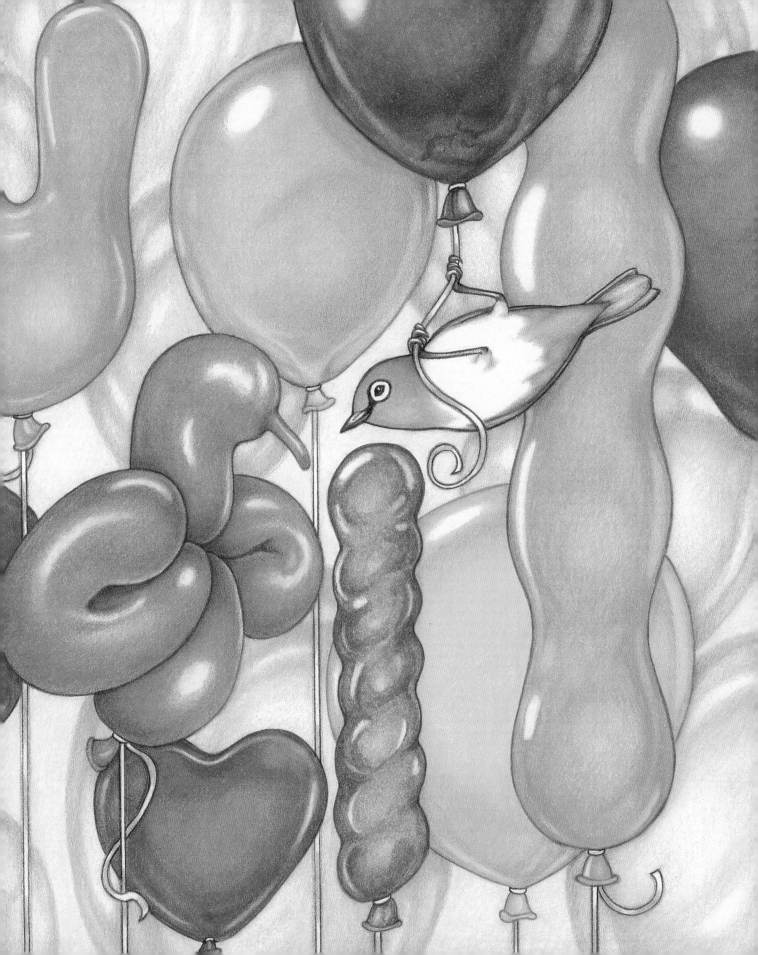

For Creative Minds

Rubber: A Natural Resource

Rubber is one of the most important raw materials in the world with thousands of uses. It is elastic, skid resistant, waterproof, bouncy, strong, holds air, keeps out noise, resists moisture, and doesn't conduct electricity.

Rubber trees are strong and tall with dark, shiny leaves. They grow at low elevations (not on mountains) in wet, tropical areas.

The first rubber trees grew in the Amazon area of Brazil and spread into other parts of South and Central America. Early European explorers took some seeds and planted them in Africa and Southeast Asia.

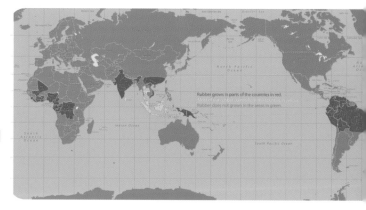

Most of the rubber that we use comes from rubber plantations in Thailand, Indonesia, and Malaysia, shown in yellow on the map. Wild rubber trees still grow in countries shown in red on the map.

Rubber plantations are far from towns, so the workers and their families live there. They have houses, schools, shops, churches, and doctors right on the plantation.

New rubber trees are planted throughout the year. Plantation workers plant seeds and then pick the healthiest saplings to plant. The rubber tree saplings are planted in rows 22 feet (6.7 m) apart with 11 feet (3.3 m) between each sapling. It only takes six or seven years for the trees to grow large enough to be tapped.

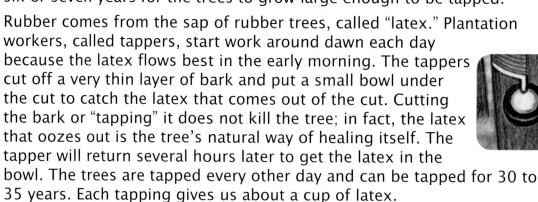

Rubber comes from the sap of rubber trees, called "latex." Plantation workers, called tappers, start work around dawn each day because the latex flows best in the early morning. The tappers cut off a very thin layer of bark and put a small bowl under the cut to catch the latex that comes out of the cut. Cutting the bark or "tapping" it does not kill the tree; in fact, the latex that oozes out is the tree's natural way of healing itself. The tapper will return several hours later to get the latex in the bowl. The trees are tapped every other day and can be tapped for 30 to 35 years. Each tapping gives us about a cup of latex.

When water is removed from the sap (latex), we get "sheet rubber."

Which of these things is made with rubber or has rubber in it?

All contain or are made from rubber: many different types of balls, latex paint, rubber O-rings, rubber bands, pencil erasers, rubber gaskets, rubber ducks, bottom of many shoes, bike and car tires, latex balloons, rubber hoses, rubber boots, rubber shower mats, rubber or latex gloves, and even rubber doormats. The number one rubber product is tires.

Balloon Sequencing

Put the balloon manufacturing events in order to unscramble the words.

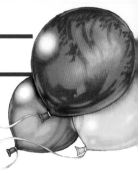

A

The latex goes into big machines to get rid of extra water.

E

In the factories, latex is mixed with a mix of chemicals and color.

F

The balloons are heated (vulcanized) to make the rubber strong.

L

A tapper gets up before dawn to gather latex from the rubber trees.

N
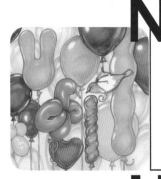
The packages are trucked to stores for you to buy and use.

T

Ships carry the latex to factories all around the world.

U

Balloons are taken off the molds, washed, dried, and put in packages to be sold.

X

Molds are dipped into colored latex and shaped into balloons.

Answer: LATEX FUN

Rubber True or False

Do you think these statements are true or false? Answers are upside down, below.

1 The first bicycle tires were made out of rubber.

2 People in Central and South America were the first people to use rubber balls.

3 Rubber erases or "rubs" out pencil markings. That is how we get the word "rubber."

4 People always knew that rubber would be used for all kinds of things.

5 The average rubber tree produces 19 pounds of latex per year.

6 Balloons have always been made from rubber.

7 Rubber trees grow in habitats all over the world.

8 When the latex rubber comes out of the tree, it is a liquid sap.

9 Charles Goodyear discovered a process called "vulcanization" that is essential for all of the rubber products that we use.

10 Vulcanization uses chemicals and heat to change the soft, sticky, taffy-like rubber into strong, elastic rubber (cured rubber).

For my good friends, Linda Joy Singleton and Linda Whalen—DS
To BK and JK, who help me soar—LAK

Thanks to Ted A. Vlamis, President, and Ted J. Vlamis, Vice President, of Pioneer Balloon Company; and to Marty Fish of the International Balloon Association for verifying the accuracy of the balloon manufacturing processes and to Jim Dryburgh, CEO and Owner of Holz Rubber Company for verifying the rubber information in this book.

Library of Congress Cataloging-in-Publication Data

Smith, Danna.
  Balloon trees / by Danna Smith ; illustrated by Laurie Allen Klein.
     pages cm
  Audience: 4-8.
  Audience: K to grade 3.
  ISBN 978-1-60718-612-0 (English hardcover) -- ISBN 978-1-60718-707-3 (Spanish hardcover) -- ISBN 978-1-60718-624-3 (English pbk.) -- ISBN 978-1-60718-636-6 (English ebook (downloadable)) -- ISBN 978-1-60718-648-9 (Spanish ebook (downloadable)) -- ISBN 978-1-60718-660-1 (interactive English/Spanish ebook (web-based)) 1. Rubber plants--Juvenile literature. 2. Rubber--Juvenile literature. I. Klein, Laurie Allen, illustrator. II. Title.
  SB290.S55 2013
  633.8'952--dc23
                         2012030119

Balloon Trees: Original Title in English
Los árboles de globos: Spanish Title Translated by Rosalyna Toth

730 Lexile Level
key phrases for educators: production of goods (how things are made), natural resources, transportation of goods, geography

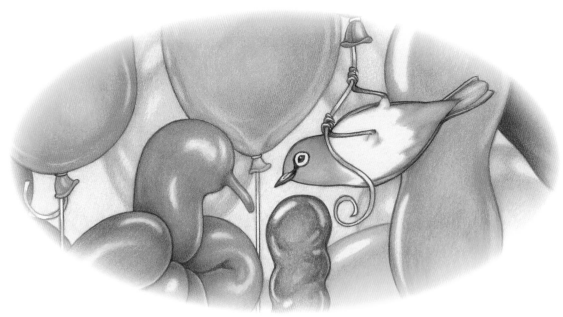

Manufactured in China, December, 2012
This product conforms to CPSIA 2008
First Printing

Sylvan Dell Publishing
Mt. Pleasant, SC 29464
www.SylvanDellPublishing.com